THE ECONOMIC STATUS
OF NEGROES

*Summary and analysis of the materials presented
at the Conference on the Economic Status of
the Negro, held in Washington, D. C.,
May 11-13, 1933, under the
sponsorship of the Julius
Rosenwald Fund.*

REPORT PREPARED FOR THE COMMITTEE ON FINDINGS

BY

CHARLES S. JOHNSON

FISK UNIVERSITY PRESS

1933

THE ECONOMIC STATUS OF NEGROES

THERE would be no reason to regard the economic status of the American Negro as any different from that of the rest of the population, or even from that of the general wage earning population, if this status were not so intricately bound up with other special social and cultural factors. These other factors are the unique historical relationship of Negroes to the development of American industry and life; the inescapable limitation of their cultural and economic expansion by the very institutions which they helped, helplessly, to create; their high visibility as a group; and the stern necessity now, in this period of economic distress, to make swift adjustment, as a conspicuous minority, to a bewilderingly complicated economic structure, if they are to survive in it.

In the midst of the most serious and sustained economic depression which this country has experienced in its history, the fact stands out clearly that the Negro working population, by far larger in proportion to its full number than is true of any other group, has also experienced vastly greater economic changes within itself. The period of our greatest national expansion witnessed, at the same time, even grosser readjustments for Negroes, both economically and culturally. There has been, for example, a rapid urbanization of the general population, but for the Negro this change has been more rapid and accomplished within a briefer period and under greater pressure. There has been accelerated national industrialization over the past fifty years, but the industrialization of Negroes, begun less than twenty years ago, has been more precipitous in its character and less certain in its goals. They have been the marginal men of industry since industry came to power; they are the marginal men of agriculture as agriculture's power declines. If this were all, the situation would still, perhaps, be no less complicated than that of men generally who by the logic of our system are expected to live meagerly. But complexity has been added by the frequent confusion of race and class. Occupations have been compartmentalized and there has been a further confusion of the factor of skill with the fact of race. The "dynamic qualities of unregulated modern life" become, thus, infinitely more dangerous and menacing for such a socially helpless group.

The policy of laissez-faire, which has for recent centuries encouraged individual enterprise and made the socialization of the gains of democracy a matter of voluntary impulse, has likewise reserved for the socially strong the power of exercising its power over the socially weak. Broad programs of economic improvement, which are well conceived and well intentioned, may seem entirely justified in assuming the Negro workers as part of the total picture and requiring no special consideration. What is commonly overlooked is the heavy inhibiting hand of tradition which too often hesitates to include these workers within the practical scope of policy and program, or fails entirely to conceive the policy as intending to encompass them. Whatever the intention of these programs, whether they be private or official, the fact remains that they reveal conspicuous unevenness in regard to the Negro population which numbers nearly twelve million.

These normal irregularities have been made acute by the present economic crisis and although the American situation is but a part of a vaster world disorganization, it is certain that there can be neither full understanding nor correction of the American angle without taking into account a situation which reflects what really amounts to the greatest defects of function in our system. From the point of view of the Negroes themselves this failure is, of course, even more serious. As one Negro student has observed regarding the present situation, not without a touch of bitterness, "one per cent makes little difference to a statistician but it spells hell to a man on the edge of starvation."

It was with the thought of making possible this essential appraisal of Negro status, and establishing a factual basis for constructive planning for the future in this regard, that the Julius Rosenwald Fund undertook to assemble as many students and active workers in this field as were known to have information useful for guidance. The membership of the Conference included white and Negro scholars of distinction in economics and sociology, representatives of all the important agencies interested in the Negro, a number of the national agencies of labor and industry, and several representatives of the governmental departments. In the planning of the Conference material aid was given by the Departments of Labor, Agriculture, and Commerce, and the sessions were held in Washington, in the rooms of the Department of the Interior.

This pamphlet is a digest and interpretation of the reports and discussions of the Conference.

WHAT IS HAPPENING TO THE NEGRO POPULATION

Although the past two decades cover the period of most violent occupational readjustment for Negroes, and, likewise, their most rápid industrialization, this period is significant more as one of acceleration of certain tendencies than as the beginning of them. To portray these extremes adequately changes should be traced over at least four decades. Monroe N. Work, of the Department of Research and Records, Tuskegee Institute, contributed to the conference analyses both of population and occupational trends for a forty-year period.

The Negro rate of population growth has been declining since 1890. If taken by itself there has been an almost 50 per cent increase in the Negro population since 1890, but their numerical importance in the population has dropped over two points (from 11.9 to 9.7). During the past ten years at least there has been a decline in the true rate of natural increase. "The rate of natural increase" is the statistician's term for a stabilized rate at which a population would grow if a given birth and death rate by age and sex continued indefinitely and no migration took place. Without migration it is doubtful if the northern Negroes could have maintained their numbers. In the South the decline can be accounted for only by assuming a drop in the specific birth rates, because the mortality rates have been falling. The death of fewer children has been the chief factor in extending expectancy of life at birth. The mortality rates of Negroes in the South, having farther to fall, register a more conspicuous decline in this section than elsewhere. The rates in the North, on the other hand, have reflected the most aggravated period of their readjustment to the new conditions of urban and industrial life. Generally considered, there are fewer young persons in the Negro population now than forty years ago.

Migration between sectional divisions of the country, but chiefly from south to north, has been increasing steadily for the past thirty years. Large cities are becoming blacker, while smaller cities and rural places are becoming whiter. Over these forty years there has been a bare 11 per cent increase of rural Negroes—less than 3 per cent a decade. But in this same period the black population of the cities has mounted 250 per cent.

The historical significance of the black belt concentrations appears to be carrying over into a concentration in industrial centers. The astonishing occupational shifts of this population over the past few years is revealed in what is happening to the black belt cotton areas. Forty years ago 56 per cent of all Negro workers were in agriculture and most of them in the Cotton Belt. In 1930 this concentration has been reduced to 36.7 per cent. Domestic service was another broad occupation which served in the towns and cities of the South the same role as agriculture in the rural areas. In forty years the Negro proportions in domestic service fell from 31.2 to 28.6. That the shift has been to industry is indicated in the rise in the percentages of these workers engaged in all jobs other than agriculture and domestic service from 13 per cent to 35 per cent. The smaller southern centers shared with the larger northern centers in drawing this labor from the farms. The proportion of Negro women in agriculture fell off nearly half (from 58.4 to 34.8) and the proportion of Negroes living in the North increased from 11.0 per cent of the total in 1910 to 21.3 per cent in 1930.

The Negro population in the whole population has declined in every southern state except Oklahoma and West Virginia as a result almost wholly of migration. West Virginia is really more a border than a southern state. Louisiana shows the widest range of change, from 50.0 per cent of the population to 36.9 per cent. There have been somewhat corresponding figures for various occupational divisions in these states, as will be noted later. According to the Scripps Foundation estimates the Negro population, which amounted to practically 11,900,000 in 1930, will increase to 13,000,000 in 1940, an increase of a little over one million, and will reach its maximum size approximately in 1970 at about 14,400,000. At the same time the total population will have reached its maximum at about 154,000,000. If the assumptions for birth and death rates hold true for the future, the 1980 population will contain 9.2 per cent Negroes instead of the 9.7 per cent as it is now.

THE SOUTH

Despite two tremendous mass migrations of Negroes from the South since 1910, drawing off over a million and a half Negroes, this section still retains four-fifths of the Negro population. The economic situation of the South thus becomes an important base for interpretation of Negro economic status. Dr. Claudius Murchison, of the University of North Carolina, has provided a summary of the South's special sectional problems. Money incomes in the South, he points out, are chronically lower by approximately one-third than the national income. The disparity applies with deadly accuracy to all groups—the mill workers, the tenant farmers, the coal miners, the iron and steel workers, the sawmill operators, school teachers and clerks. Whether the economic status be judged by money earnings, by bank savings, by building and loan assets, by ownership of automobiles and radios, by family budget exhibits, or by expenditures for books and magazines, all findings converge upon the one conclusion that the large majority is barely above a minimum of subsistence level, even in so-called normal times.

In such a community it is likely that a given decline in incomes, over the short run, will work a more generalized havoc than in a community where prosperity means comfortable margins for savings and luxuries. In abnormal periods the section experiences about the same degree of contraction, but the significance of this contraction is more serious. Dr. Murchison was referring to the entire population of the South, not specifically to the Negro population, which in turn is on a considerably lower level of subsistence than the section as a whole.

The recent southern business recession actually began a year in advance of the national business curve. Economics of the South, designed primarily for production of goods which are not foodstuffs for export, and the importation of foodstuffs, are such that a decline in incomes is widespread and immediate in its effect.

Among the manufacturing industries in the South, the iron and steel industry has been most seriously affected. The southern division of the textile industry has maintained physical volume but only with demoralization of prices, wages and employment, with profits non-existent. Increased mechanization and the "stretch-out systems" in textiles have reduced employment more rapidly than they have reduced production, and wages have declined at a still more rapid pace. In this typically southern industry may be found individualism with little modification, and at its worst.

The tobacco industry, well organized and integrated, has been relatively stable with less than a 20 per cent decline in consumption, and profits still possible. Ninety per cent of the former lumber markets had dried up in 1932. Coal mining and the production of petroleum have been sustained in physical volume, but price and wage demoralization has been greater than in industries suffering even larger curtailment of volume.

The South's population, white and Negro, has been in the past relatively immobile. In recent years, however, as a result of growing disorganization in agriculture, there have been startling shifts from rural to urban centers within and from states which for decades have never been seriously affected by migration.

PRESENT POSITION OF NEGROES
IN BASIC INDUSTRIES

It has been impossible to escape the devastating influence of the introduction of machinery on a large scale into certain industries, and the recent extraordinary increase in management efficiency. Both of these have had their effect in reducing the volume of man power generally. Greatest inroads have been made in the unskilled lines, which provide, incidentally, no less than 75 per cent of the Negro industrial jobs. Since 1870, one-fourth of the nation's active labor power has been released from the processes of physical production by application of science and technology to production.

The movement cityward of the great reserves of agricultural workers, white and Negro, has added to the complexity of the industrial situation. Only 21 per cent of the working population were needed in 1930 to supply the food for the nation, which six decades ago required half of the workers. There have been competition, contraction, and finally suspension of a large part of industrial activity with consequent unemployment on a scale both monumental and disrupting.

The fate of the Negro workers in these changing tides has been uneven, not to say uncertain, generally. The effort to estimate this status was, of necessity, restricted in the Conference to a selected group of the basic industries which would yield some comparative figures over a reasonable period. These analyses were made by persons whose acquaintance with special industries gave to their estimates a measure of authority.

Trends in other industries are noted generally in this memorandum by way of supplementing the list of industries significant for Negro workers.

COAL MINING

Bituminous coal mining is a sick industry. The peak of coal production was reached in 1918. Regardless of the decreased demand for coal after 1918 the productive capacity continued to increase for five years. Gradual retrenchment began in 1923 to make the inevitable adjustment of production to demand. In 1930 coal production was at the lowest level since 1904. In the absence of any effective regulation, state or federal, the price system has been the sole regulator of production. Over-development is due not only to the increase in the production in coal but to increased competition with coal substitutes, such as oil, natural gas and water power.

The number of miners increased every year from 1890 to 1923 and has decreased every year since 1923. The decrease in the number of miners employed since 1923 is due to a decreased demand for coal, and to the increase in output per man. Between 1920 and 1929 the number of bituminous coal mining companies decreased 26.5 per cent, and this decrease occurred, for the most part, in medium sized companies.

Despite the stubborn resistance of the mining industry to mechanization, machines are, nevertheless, responsible for the recent increase in output per man, and for a considerable amount of technological unemployment. On the basis of the present demand for coal and the present output per man over 200.000 miners need to be withdrawn from the industry if those remaining are to extricate themselves from the intolerably low wage standards which now prevail. Assuming that the productive capacity of the mines should be great enough to meet the 1929 requirements for coal, this industry has from 50 per cent to 75 per cent greater capacity than is necessary to meet the demands of the market. Stabilization can be achieved, only by reducing productive capacity to a level with normal demand.

In 1920 about 8 per cent of the bituminous coal miners in the United States were Negroes. They were massed chiefly in the Alabama coal fields in which 52 7 per cent of the miners were Negroes. In West Virginia 19.9 per cent of the miners were Negroes, and in Kentucky about 20 per cent. In 1930 the number of Negro miners in Alabama had doubled but their percentage to the total decreased 5 per cent. Negro miners were 13.6 per cent of all miners in Kentucky and 21 8 per cent of all miners in West Virginia They have a greater degree of security in their jobs in the mines than in most other industries, due to the prevailing custom of employing the whole labor force whenever the mines operate, and shutting down the mines completely except for a few maintenance men, when there are no orders for coal.

Complete mechanization of a mine alters the policy of internal labor organization, thus depriving the miner of a considerable part of his traditional freedom Negro miners have not as yet experienced the inroads of mechanization to any considerable extent except in Alabama where, incidentally, they have had their largest proportions.

[9]

Since coal is produced mechanically at a lower cost, at least in the central competitive field, it is inevitable that it will come in competition with the coal mined in southern territory. The competition may be expected to result in loss of orders, in forcing down the wage scale, and eventually in compelling the further mechanization of the southern mines.

FOOD PRODUCTS

The food products industry is the country's biggest single business and is at the same time the most stable business in the depression. Only banking and public utilities have exceeded food and kindred products in the matter of sustaining its payrolls. In the most prosperous years Negroes have had only small numbers in this field. Those employed have been for the most part engaged in such unskilled tasks as cleaners and porters. This practice applies to practically all of the nationally known prepared and branded foods.

A notable exception in the matter of employment is the meat packing industry, in which the work, while disagreeable, has a moderate range of skill The Chicago, St Louis, Kansas City and Omaha abattoirs have made use of Negro labor in large numbers. Reductions in the working force due to the depression have in general left these Negro workers in relatively larger proportions than other workers. Four meat packing plants in Omaha counted Negro employment as 9 5 per cent of their total in 1930, and in 1923, with but 45 per cent of their former total force, 15 per cent were Negroes. In Kansas City the proportion of Negroes employed in the meat packing industry ranged from 11 per cent at the Cudahy plant to 30 per cent at the Armour plant In the meat packing industry in the St Louis district, however, Negroes have been reduced both in numbers and in their proportion to the total workers

The prospects and estimates of new employment following the re-opening of breweries for the manufacture of beer of increased alcoholic content, have not been fulfilled with reference to either white or Negro workers Actual numbers employed are much below the figures anticipated for whites and no change has occurred in the practice of brewers' unions of excluding Negroes from membership and consequently from employment. In St Louis, Negroes were not employed in the past, and there is no indication of future employment. In Louisville they are used only as janitors and laborers. In Pittsburgh, where union men only are employed, there are only four Negro members in the district. The same situation was found to hold for Baltimore, Newark, Seattle, Fort Wayne, and Denver.

In certain southern cities where Negro truck drivers and helpers have been used in distribution of such food products as ice and milk, they have been displaced to make room for white combination driver-salesmen.

SKILLED CRAFTS

Negroes have a history in the skilled trades beginning with the founding of the American colonies. Their position in these trades, in the new industrial direction and emphasis, has seriously declined in importance. While contributing 9.6 per cent of the population and 6 3 per cent of the workers in manufacturing and mechanical industries, they are as yet but 3.1 per cent of the workers in important skilled crafts Their greatest numerical importance at present is in those crafts which are waning, and their smallest unit concentrations are in the fields of new industrial emphasis. The greatest single loss, over the past decade, has been in the number of carpenters, a condition which reflects both technological improvement and displacement by white workers, largely on racial grounds. However, the rate of Negro increase in old line trades, considered as a whole, is twice as rapid as the increase for all workers Significantly, the older concentrations of Negro skilled workers are being broken up, scattering Negro workers in smaller numbers over more fields.

Negro artisans and craftsmen until very recently have been almost wholly in the South. The lines in which they have been developing have been declining due to the general tendency of such work to be concentrated in factories, and to recent techno. logical changes. Inclusion of Negroes in the new industrial organization has been uneven and slow because of the location of most of these factories in the South, because of the coming of women into industry, the lag in the urbanization of Negroes, and the large scale use of foreign-born workers. Changes in building methods now require new types of workers. The importance of carpenters and draftsmen in the building industry has, thus, been diminished. Machinists, who represent a highly organized craft, the unions of which bar Negroes, increased enormously between 1890 and 1920, but experienced a sudden general decline between 1920 and 1930.

Since 1890 Negro skilled workers have gained in masonry, iron working and stationary engineering, and lost ground in carpentry, plastering, brick and tile making, marble and stone cutting, blacksmithing, wheelwrighting, boot and shoe making, harness and saddle making, leather currying and tanning. The decline of carpenters in five southern states, which, incidentally, have been the slowest to introduce technological improvements in the building operations, reveals direct displacement by white workers. This is equally true of bricklayers and contractors in many of these cities. Negro artisans and building trade craftsmen provide only one third of their population proportion.

The most consistent losses of Negro artisans, however, are in the crafts which are themselves waning in importance, such as blacksmithing, coopering, and shoe making Carpentry is the outstanding exception. The rate of decrease in Negro bricklayers, roofers and slaters, electricians, plasterers, building contractors, has been less than the total rate, while the increase of Negro plumbers, painters, and cement finishers has been greater than the total rate, although actual numbers have been small Negro molders increased while all other molders declined. White tool makers increased while Negro tool makers declined. The rate of increase for all skilled workers was slightly higher than the Negro increase In the waning or dying crafts the rate of decline of the total is twice that of Negroes, suggesting a slower readjustment of these Negroes to the new industrial shifts The increase in skilled occupations of Negroes is due chiefly to their industrialization following northward migration from 1917 to 1922.

CONSTRUCTION

The largest concentration of Negroes under manufacturing and mechanical industries is to be found in building construction. The most important decline in building activity has been in residential construction on which Negroes have found greatest employment. The highest recorded unemployed group of American workers revealed in the 1930 census was that of building laborers They showed an unemployment rate four times that of all other workers. But the census was taken before the trough of the depression was reached. Estimates in 1932 based upon special studies in sections, showed four times as many unemployed as in 1930.

Important technological changes making for enormous labor displacement have been made both in the building and road construction industry. While there have been consistent increases in both skilled and unskilled Negro workers in building construction this is a field which, measured in terms of unemployment, has suffered most violently of all large industries from seasonal and cyclical depressions, and from technological development.

STEEL

In 1920 Negroes were 5 8 per cent of all employees in iron, steel, and machinery industries. In 1930 total employment in iron, steel, and machinery industries fell off 12 per cent, but there was a fractional increase in the Negro percentage of total workers from 6 6 per cent to 6 8 per cent. This increase, however, was not consistent for all types of work in this field. The total number of laborers and operatives in the iron and steel industry, however, remained constant for the last decade. In this industry, on the 1926 base there is revealed a reduction of employment by one-half and of earnings by three-fourths.

The "durable goods" industries suffer wide fluctuations in value in the business cycle. Negro industrial employment is concentrated in those fields of durable goods production that have been most seriously curtailed. Unemployment, as has been noted generally, has been more severe among unskilled laborers than among other groups. This unemployment in the steel industries in more normal times, is less among the foreign-born whites than among Negroes, and less among Negroes than among native whites, due, no doubt, to the character of the work and to the available native white labor supply for these unskilled jobs. The increase in unemployment among laborers, however, between April, 1930, and January, 1931, was greatest among Negroes, the foreign-born coming next, and the native whites last. This is evidently a reflection of increased competition. In the four occupations containing the bulk of the steel workers the foreign-born whites showed greatest unemployment, while the Negroes and native whites ranked next with approximately the same proportions of unemployed persons.

TRADE AND TRANSPORTATION

A significant fact about Negro occupations in recent years is the increasingly wide distribution over many fields, although only a few of these fields (and usually those fields traditionally associated with Negroes), have as yet any important numerical concentrations. Thus it happens that large increases or decreases may appear for specific occupations which, though in point of total workers have little importance, yet are important signals for the Negro group itself. One or two hundred Negro workers in an entirely new line thus become important as an index of industrial penetration, and of versatility although their proportions to the total workers are not sufficient to provoke mass opposition. Frequently this is due to the unimportance or declining importance of the occupation itself.

Since 1890 Negro hucksters and peddlers, retail dealers, undertakers, teamsters, hostlers, and mail carriers have increased their proportions slightly. Commercial travellers, boatmen and canalmen, locomotive firemen, chauffeurs, railway mail clerks, laborers, porters and helpers in stores and messengers have lost ground by a wider margin than is represented in the increase in other lines.

The cold figures on decline in railway transportation conceal such significant tangents as the sustained tragedy of Negro locomotive firemen whose numbers have been decreased by murders committed by white men wanting their jobs, who thought Negroes should not be locomotive firemen, but could not force them out by threats or compel the companies employing them to scrap their records of service. Chauffeuring is one of the relatively new occupations, falling between the coachman's role and the new mechanical art of motoring, it has been a marginal occupation, as likely to fall to Negroes as to any others. The declining importance of Negroes in this occupation is serious because of the large numbers represented and because of the manifest willingness of other workers to compete strenuously in what is virtually a personal service field. Just as significant, however, is the relative loss in importance of Negro laborers, porters and helpers in stores and messengers. These jobs were a few decades ago almost wholly in their hands.

DOMESTIC SERVICE

If agriculture and domestic service were taken together they would account for 60 per cent of the Negroes gainfully employed. Domestic service has been for the most part a personal arrangement of a household with a servant. The work, by its very nature, has been regulated only by the will of the employer and the willingness of the servant. It is as a rule poorly paid, but despite this, has offered a measure of security in such employment as it happened to be Normally it is little affected by seasonal fluctuations or by depressions of brief duration. The widespread and sustained business depression with consequent loss of earnings of employers has forced dispensing with many servants, and sent many jobless white persons seeking for the first time these traditional Negro jobs. A result is that the proportions of Negroes in domestic service generally have declined in spite of the fact that nearly a quarter of a million Negro women have had to abandon agriculture, with domestic service as their most logical next field of employment. There have been decreases in the proportion of Negroes in domestic service in ten of the fifteen southern states West Virginia, Tennessee, Alabama, Maryland and Oklahoma were the exceptions. These five states, however, permitted a large enough expansion to overcome losses in the other ten and leave a margin of about 10 per cent improvement over the forty years.

PROFESSIONS

Professional classes among Negroes increased 69 per cent between 1920 and 1930. The problem in professional classes is not one of over-population but of maldistribution.   As summarized by Ira DeA. Reid of the National Urban League: there exists a popular conception that professional occupations among Negroes are over-crowded. This is not true. Though 136,000 Negroes are employed in all professional occupations, the race is understaffed in all fields save that of the ministry. The problem in the professions is not one of over-population, but one of maldistribution. Our professional classes increased from 34,000 in 1890 to 135,000 in 1930. The rate of increase for persons in this class was twice as rapid during the decade 1920-1930— 69 per cent—as during the period 1910-1920, when they increased 31 per cent. In the technical fields, there has been a marked advance, particularly in the field of chemistry and metallurgy, where the number of technicians among Negroes increased twice as rapidly as in the white group. Mining, civil, electrical and mechanical engineers increased 90 per cent during the 1920-1930 decade, while the total number increased approximately 65 per cent. Architects, draftsmen and designers, on the other hand, showed a slight increase.

The medical profession increased rapidly from 1900-1910, but much less rapidly from 1920-1930, failing to keep pace with the population growth. In fact, since 1910 there has been a relative decline in the number of physicians—both white and black On the other hand, there has been a twelve-fold increase in the number of Negro dentists who now number approximately 1,700.

Of growing importance is the employment of librarians, social workers, actors, artists and musicians. In 1930 each of these groups showed increases of more than half of their total 1920 occupancy. Actors increased more than 100 per cent. The motion picture industry gave employment through Hollywood's Central Casting Bureau. Social workers increased from 1,200 in 1920 to 2,400 in 1930. Musicians and teachers of music, riding the crest of the popular demand for syncopated rhythm, increased from 5,700 to 11,500, or about three times as rapidly as did musicians in the white group.

Teachers and clergymen, representing the older individual professions, assumed greater numerical importance in the last decade. College presidents and professors, now numbering approximately 1,100, increased more than 100 per cent, while teachers increased 53 3 per cent. Both of these increases were more rapid among Negroes than among whites. Clergymen who had noted relative declines in the rate of growth of their profession since the 1890-1900 decade (when the number increased by 27 per cent and a drop to 15 per cent in 1900-1910 to 8 per cent in 1910-1920) took heart in seeing their greatest increase of the century—28 per cent—occur in the last census decade. They remained proportionately more numerous among the Negro population than among any other racial group, and the 25,000 Negroes so engaged in 1930 formed 17 per cent of all the country's clergymen.

Women are approximately 45 per cent of the entire Negro professional classes, being four-fifths of all school teachers, librarians, social and welfare workers, one-half of the actors and artists, and they monopolize the field of trained nurses. In the single field of the ministry Negroes have fewer persons per professional than the white population In comparing the ratios for the six leading professions among Negroes with the ratios for the same professions among the white population, it appears that there are twice as many persons per teacher among Negroes, four times as many persons per nurse, four-and-one-half times as many persons per dentist, fifteen times as many persons per lawyer, and only half as many persons per clergyman as for the white population

NEGRO BUSINESS

There is yet considerable confusion as to the direct objective and possibility of development of Negro business as a distinct economy. It is thought of by Negroes first as an avenue for employment for themselves both as owners and workers In a sense it is a protest development against discriminations both in the matter of private employment and public accommodation. Having the greatest cause for cooperative economic techniques, and perhaps greatest grounds for protest against unrestrained individualism, these Negro enterprises have not only shown least capacity for cooperative ventures, but seem to have been guided in their business aspirations by the general type of business successes against which they have deepest complaint on behalf of

Negro workers generally. Some 25,000 of these small Negro enterprises during 1929 averaged net sales of $3,935, and gave employment to 12,561 persons, mostly Negroes. The effect upon employment, thus, is negligible.

Negro retail dealers increased 20 per cent between 1920 and 1930, but most of these businesses were small, precarious and frequently wasteful enterprises. Restaurants, cafes, lunch rooms, and lodging houses increased by one-third. This is a form of personal service socially related to the discriminatory practices which Negroes experience generally. Hotels showed not actual numerical increase but there was a wider geographical distribution. Positions of management in manufacturing and mechanical enterprises, automotive transportation, and insurance showed large percentage gains, but upon a small numerical basis.

The commercial classes among Negroes increased 9 per cent and the total number of workers so employed increased by one-third. The Negro financial group, which includes banks and insurance companies, doubled between 1920 and 1930, and clerical employment increased 18 per cent. Since 1928, however, Negro banking has suffered tragic losses, but these have been losses which paralleled the general trend in financial institutions. The insurance companies likewise have lost in the volume of their business and in lapsed policies. In general, it appears that the Negro middle class has shown "increased economic vitality and some improvement in its economic status over the last two decades." The chief evidence of this improvement, however, is a more conspicuous consumption. These enterprises are faced with the difficulty of a clientele of small incomes and "the merciless and almost inescapable competition of white business and organized corporations with endless capital."

While large business concerns still hesitate to take Negroes into the "white collar" jobs of their establishments, the absorptive power of Negro business itself for Negro workers is extremely low.

THE FEDERAL GOVERNMENT AS EMPLOYER

Although uncertainties of individual policy among employers may explain the uncertainty of status of Negroes in American industries, these workers have perhaps fared better at the hands of private employers than at the hands of the Federal Government. This observation can be made despite the frequency of exploitation of labor by private employers, and the use of Negro labor as an aid in this exploitation. As T. Arnold Hill points out, "aside from the Post Office in which they have not had access to all branches, Negroes have had very little share in the operation or work of the Federal Government." Negro mail carriers more than doubled the average increase for all mail carriers, but railway mail clerks lost almost 20 per cent of their number as the field itself showed a gain of 10 per cent in workers Such vast federal prospects as Boulder Dam and the various river projects supplying thousands with work have included relatively few Negro workers. The new bureaus created under federal control which have been absorbing some of the excess labor have likewise engaged negligible numbers of Negroes. The recent reforestation program into which a clause was inserted against discrimination, has found it exceedingly difficult to overcome the habit of discrimination as soon as the administration is transferred to the southern states and counties. The practice has not been general but common enough to cause concern over the failure of the ultimate conservator of the security of the country's least protected workers.

Not all of the exclusion is due to chance. To the testimony of statisticians may be added the observation of Professor Kelly Miller, who attributed to simple race prejudice the thwarting of the Federal Government's obligation to serve its black citizens. "Race prejudice," he said, "fixes the Negro at the lower level of service in the Federal Government. I am pretty well acquainted with the Civil Service Commission, and with one of the members who is retiring, and he tells me that it is practically impossible for a Negro, though he be as wise as Einstein, to receive a clerkship in the Federal Government. The Negro is assigned in the federal service to the Post Office, for the most part, for there the labor is not wholly clerical, but essentially manual." As a further illustration of types of difficulty encountered, when announcement was made of work to begin on bridge construction under R F C. funds, in Louisiana, it was stipulated that only registered voters would be employed There are few Negro registered voters in the state and this scarcity has been accomplished by means well known to those who have studied the illegal Negro disfranchisement in most of the states of the South.

LABOR UNION PRACTICE

One of the striking anomalies of the Negro's economic predicament is the attitude of his fellows in a working class situation which adds racial group competition to the bitter individual struggle for a livelihood. While much of the failure of inclusion of Negroes under such protection as the unions may guarantee is due to their previous elimination from organized fields, and to the general lack of organization in fields of greatest Negro labor concentration, the fact remains that direct exclusion is a widespread practice. Dr. Paul Douglas, in consideration of the general situation of Negro non-membership in unions, felt that it was nevertheless possible to exaggerate the degree to which formal union restrictions have deprived Negroes of jobs, since the unions actually represent in these organizations not more than 10 per cent of the normal number of industrial workers. It was pointed out, however, that this 10 per cent is actually dominating and includes the most highly paid crafts. Moreover, there has been a disposition on the part of the administration to give important recognition to the unions in a partnership with Government itself. Such new importance gives acute emphasis to the practice of exclusion of Negroes or discouragement of membership where such membership is not actually barred. Whether or not labor can live up to the responsibility is still an open question and a challenge is presented not only to its capacity for swift and effective reorganization from a craft to an industrial basis, but to a reorganization of its attitudes toward the black workers who are the ultimate test of a thoroughgoing labor policy.

NEGRO WOMEN IN INDUSTRY

The role of the Negro woman in the family has been one of historical note. During slavery and for years afterwards she was the strongest force in the Negro family and, under the shifting fortunes of the group, played a vital part in guaranteeing a means of security in their living. She has, thus, been a wage earner on a large scale longer than the women of other groups and within her family the necessity has been more compelling.

Negro women are 9.7 per cent of the woman population 10 years of age and over, but are 17.1 per cent of employed women. This is nearly double her share. Thirty eight and nine tenths per cent of Negro women are employed as compared with 20 3 per cent white women. In the past ten years there has been a rapid growth of numbers employed, but a slight increase in their proportions to the total, suggesting the pressure of these times on all families, which is forcing more white women into service. Some of this change, moreover, represents displacement by these white women.

In 1930 the two great occupation groups employing most of the Negro women were domestic and personal service and agriculture. In agriculture they decreased in the last decade and increased 5 8 per cent in domestic and personal service This gain was not as great as that of native white women. Negro women increased by one-third in clerical work, and by one-fourth in trade. In professional occupations they increased 60 9 per cent as compared with 49 6 per cent for white women This turnover is largely in the number of school teachers. One woman teacher in every twenty in 1930 was a Negro

Dressmakers and seamstresses, who are not working in factories, constituted one-half of the Negro women in manufacturing. The next largest group was in cigar and tobacco plants These occupations declined between 1920 and 1930 Nearly one-fourth of the women in cigar factories in 1930 were Negroes. Increase in clothing industries amounted to 103 6 per cent for Negro women, and 38 6 per cent for white women, while in food products Negro women gained to the extent of 43 per cent while white women increased 19 9 per cent

Just as they have ranked high in the number of wage earners, they have bulked large among the unemployed when work became scarce In Brooklyn and Manhattan, New York, 28 5 per cent of those who worked were out of work, and in Detroit 75 per cent of them were idle. More than 40 per cent were unemployed in Chicago, Houston, St Louis, Philadelphia and Cleveland. Invariably they showed highest unemployment rates of all working women Recent unemployment studies in Baltimore showed Negro women 17 3 per cent of the population, 29 6 per cent of those normally gainfully employed, and 27 5 per cent of the unemployed Studies in Philadelphia showed them 11 1 per cent of the population, 17 4 per cent normally employed, and 28 17 per cent of the unemployed.

THE POSITION GENERALLY

The figures show unevenness in occupational gains and losses. There are gains in industries at the cost of wage standards, losses in new fields, a surprising steadiness in marginal occupations, either gains or a strange conservatism about leaving dying crafts, a precipitous rush to the most precarious of American industries, loss of traditional occupations, and small gains over a wide distribution of unaccustomed jobs. On the whole their status is marginal, although they reflect in practically every movement the general course of the industries. There is a surprisingly small amount of purely racial displacement, but where the crust of tradition has been broken it has most often been broken downward to admit other workers into such jobs as Negroes have pinned their security upon. As measured statistically there has been enough gain to permit Mr. Monroe N. Work to say:

> "The rise of the status of a group can be measured to some degree by the extent to which the members of the group gainfully occupied are entering into those occupations requiring some skill, initiative, experience and special training. It has been seen . . . that the number of Negroes is increasing in these classes of occupations. One can ask whether, by such a test, we may but conclude that the economic status of the Negro is tending to rise."

As measured statistically from another angle, there has been so little gain as to permit Dr. W. E. B. DuBois to say, with an equal conviction:

> ". . . during fifty years there is no doubt that we have failed in our main objectives. . . . We must acknowledge that after an effort of a half century, despite what we have undoubtedly accomplished and essayed, we are not recognized as an integral part of American civilization, or of modern culture. We have found the main wall of race prejudice impenetrable. We have done a great deal, without doubt; in spite of a bad and incomplete school system we have learned in large measure to read and write. Our progress in art and literature, in science, even in business, has been notable. Our determined opening of labor opportunities is astounding. Our greatest failure is inability to earn a decent living. . . . As a people we are on the narrow ridge of economic survival and we know it. We are the surplus laborer without security of job or certainty of relief."

THE TRAIL OF THE DEPRESSION

What has gone before has been a tracing of the fluctuations in the industrial status of Negroes, a charting of economic gains and losses over the past few decades, but with a measure of stress upon the last period. The statistical basis ended in 1930, only one year after the close of an era of unprecedented American inflation and prosperity. The unemployment census of that year showed only 5 per cent of the population jobless. The Negro rates were characteristically higher, but they were managing to live without conspicuous distress on that low level of subsistence to which their usual circumstances had accustomed them to make adjustment. Two years after the 1930 census, sample studies reported in the voluminous and valuable report on *Recent Social Trends*, indicate that no less than 20 per cent of the working population was unable to find work. Where these studies have included Negroes the same startling excesses in unemployment have been shown.

The most recent and, without doubt, the most authentic of the unemployment studies is that conducted in Philadelphia under the direction of Dr. Joseph H. Willits of the University of Pennsylvania. With his assistants in the Industrial Research Department, Dr. Willits checked the factor of unemployment among several groups in Philadelphia for the four years 1929, 1931, 1932 and 1933, thus tracing the impact of unemployment upon the same group in the same locality over successive years. In 1929 when 9.0 per cent of all white employables were unemployed, 15.7 per cent of the Negroes were unemployed. In 1930 it was 13.8 per cent for whites and 19.4 per cent for Negroes; in 1931 it was 24.1 per cent for whites and 35.0 per cent for Negroes; and in 1932 it was 39.7 per cent for whites and 56.0 per cent for Negroes!

From the beginning of the unemployment period, the Negroes have shown a larger percentage of unemployment than the whites, but as the depression continued the percentage by which the Negro ratio exceeded that of the white tended to narrow slightly. Nevertheless in 1930 the percentage of Negroes still unemployed was half as high again as the whites. If to these proportions the 20 per cent doing part time work had been added, the unemployment rates would have been tragic as well as startling.

In the matter of made work in the city, which offered another unemployment index, actually more Negroes were counted among the applicants than there were Negroes in the city's gainfully employed occupations. The question of willingness or inability to work did not enter and has never been raised. For 90 per cent of the Negro unemployment was due to being "laid off" or as a result of firms bankrupt, merged or moved away.

The marginality of these workers is further reflected in the industrial histories of the unemployed secured by the Industrial Research Bureau. The average length of the longest job of Negroes was 3.8 years as compared with 6 years for whites. Earnings of whites were $5.00 to $10.00 more weekly in the same general labor classification, the median savings, before losing their jobs, $86.00 for Negroes and

$204.00 for whites. Nearly twice as many Negroes as whites were in arrears on their rents, a third more of the whites could get loans and just twice as much in amount and, finally, as the climax of this impact in appeals for public relief, in 1931-32, while they were 20 per cent of the city's unemployed, 27 per cent of the children under relief care were Negroes.

An extensive analysis of the effect of the depression on the Negro family has been made by Dr. E. Franklin Frazier of Fisk University.

The Negro's standard of living has been affected seriously by this unemployment as revealed in congested housing, dissipation of savings, loss of homes, of furniture, insurance and of clothes. Some of the families living near the subsistence level may have drawn a grain of profit from this extremity by having social agencies determining their diet more scientifically. This is, however, of small significance when the greater problem of malnutrition in the vast bulk of their families is considered.

The unfavorable effects upon family unity and morale have been indicated in the addition of relatives and strangers to the family group, the necessity of sending children to relatives and friends; increases in desertions and juvenile delinquency; and a loss of work habits, especially on the part of men, together with a loss of the spirit to carry on the determined struggle which the competitive life of our cities requires.

Discussion of the social disorganization forced upon the Negroes by the pressure of economic stress has at hand abundant documentation. Dr. M. O. Bousfield's reference to Negro health problems incident to low and lowered incomes is one of these. But no more seems necessary to give point to the stern circumstances of life, for which their low level of income is largely responsible, but which give rise to that complex of poor housing and homes, high mortality, low literacy, and confused social philosophy commonly referred to as the "Negro problem."

THE PLIGHT OF THE NEGRO FARM WORKER

About one-third of the Negroes working are in agriculture. Such a proportion gives immense significance to changes in this field. It is all the more important because Negro workers, despite recent trends cityward have been almost altogether rural people. Now that the cities are glutted with labor, much of which can never be absorbed, and the overburdened relief agencies are urging a return to the farm, or to any place beyond their harassed responsibility, the condition of agriculture and its prospects will, no doubt, determine largely what will happen both in its own province and in industrial centers.

The approach to this problem indicated its enormous ramifications. One unmistakable observation, whatever the approach, was that the entire field is profoundly unsettled, and agriculture, one of the most essential fields of labor, is not now profitable. "In general," says Dr. O. E. Baker, in Recent Social Trends, "American agriculture has been of an exploitative character. The conquest of a virgin continent by a fecund people governed by the spirit of laissez-faire could not have resulted in any other kind of agriculture." One result has been wasteful and enormous soil depletion' But despite this depletion agricultural production has been greater during the past decade than ever before. As in coal mining, machinery and methods have improved so rapidly that a surplus has developed, both of people and of products.

A decreasing proportion of the population engaged in full time farming is able now to produce plenty for everyone in the nation to eat. There has been, as a consequence of these pressures, an inescapable forcing out of farm people to the cities. Farm areas have contracted or shifted, the value of farm lands has suffered heavily, and there is a persistent surplus of farm products carrying prices so low that a decent living is difficult for even the best of farmers. A reflection of this is in the increased ratio of mortgage debts to value of farm real estate and the consequent foreclosures. With this has come tax increases and tax delinquencies, and either an enlarged tenant population or migration and calamitous sacrifice of farms.

If this is the situation of agriculture generally, little is required of the imagination in the matter of Negro farmers President Benjamin F. Hubert of the Georgia State College for Negroes has drawn these special problems into focus in a study of Negro agricultural status in four southern states, South Carolina, Georgia, Alabama and Mississippi. These four states had a Negro population of 2,139,748 and 75 per cent of the cultivable land in the single crop of cotton. The Negro land owners in these states decreased 17 per cent between 1920 and 1930, and tenants decreased 10 per cent.

European and Asiatic countries which have been our best markets are narrowing their demand for American grown cotton, due to the expansion of foreign producing regions. Domestic consumption seems to have reached the saturation point. Much of the land now in cotton at the margin, or near the margin, will go out of production because it is unprofitable to farm it. Since 1920 the average production of cotton per acre in these states has been approximately 176 pounds of lint, costing an average of $31 65 per bale to produce. Its value fluctuated from $38.72 in 1924 to $15.84 in 1930. At least one-third of the total acreage now being planted in cotton in these states must eventually be diverted to other uses than cotton growing. These four states, taken as a whole, represent a deficit area for most of the principal food and feed crops.

Much was heard of the plight of the farm long before the effects of the depression became widespread. Georgia alone has lost 200,000 Negroes in the past ten years, principally farmers. When the collapse in prices came the farmers were tragically overwhelmed and with effects of widespread consequences. Mr. W. W. Alexander and his research assistant, Dr. Arthur Raper, who have been making inquiries in selected counties in Mississippi and Alabama, report that in 1932 in Mississippi alone 7,000,000 acres, or more than one-sixth of the state's total agriculture acreage, was being advertised for taxes. The only check upon this extraordinary abandonment of farms out of desperation has been the inability of other farmers to buy the lands even at the sacrifice prices.

Dr. Raper observes that mortgage loans in Alabama and Georgia are made on condition that the borrower waive his homestead rights to the minimum of $300.00. At present only the very best lands are being taken over by creditors. With the depression unabated, buyers are fewer for delinquent tax lands, and for these lands taken over by the county there have been few sales.

It was inevitable that under such a generally archaic system questionable practices should flourish. In the plantation credit system, for example, the creditor storekeepers may charge any prices they choose for items, make any entries they like, collect whatever interest is wanted, and name the price to be paid tenants for farm produce with which he repays his debts. Seizure of salable produce for tenants' debts is not uncommon but there is less of it done when prices are low than when they are high.

The big plantations with their cash crops utilize the most productive land, and the masses of agricultural workers in these areas are very dependent and very poor. Small farms are usually located on relatively unproductive land, but the people living there are more independent and self-sufficing. They constitute such as there is of a rural middle-class. There is some hope that present rural depression, in making black belt land relatively less valuable for exploitative purposes, may result in less of a driving interest on the part of landlords, and consequently more independence and self direction on the part of the tenants. At present much of the land devoted to other than cotton crops is being kept in production at small annual costs rather than suffer a complete loss of the original investment by abandonment

COTTON

Considering the preeminence of cotton as the concern and, virtually, the sole dependence of the majority of Negro farmers, the general condition of cotton raising inspires little confidence in this phase of the agricultural future. There is a dismal realism in the general view of this situation as presented by Dr. E. E. Lewis of Howard University. Thirteen million bales came from American cotton farmers last year only to be added to world stocks of unused American cotton previously grown, amounting to thirteen million more bales. On January 1, 1933, these 26,000,000 bales were still waiting to be sold to textile mills here and abroad. This vast unused surplus is seldom given due weight in the expectation of immediate price raising through the reduction of cotton acreages. Even if the government could perform such an economic miracle as to restrict acreage to 8 per cent of the 1932 level, and even if nature and high fertilizer prices kept the average yield down at the low level of 150 pounds per acre, there would still be produced 9,000,000 bales annually. Seven million bales was the American consumption in the peak of prosperity, leaving 2,000,000 bales for sale abroad. But any appreciable sales inevitably bind the domestic price to the world price.

There seems no present basis for the popular hope that increased foreign demand will express itself in both increased buying and higher prices. Indeed, the world is less than ever dependent upon American grown cotton. Russia, for example, is out of the market because she can now supply her own needs completely. India, Chile, Brazil, Egypt and other scattered African areas produced 10,000,000 bales in 1931. The threat of increased world competition is a very real one.

What is of greater concern for black belt Negro farmers is the shifting of the cotton area to the Southwest—to Texas, New Mexico and neighboring territory—which, because of their topography will lend themselves more readily to mechanization. Any increase in the mechanization of cotton production will stimulate this shift. It is a movement not only away from the old Cotton Belt but away from the Negro as well.

CREDIT

Credit plays a vital role in agriculture. It is necessary for the conduct of the farming enterprise. Data concerning the uses and availability of credit for Negro farmers are meager and limited to a few local studies. One of the most important of these studies was made in North Carolina by Dr. Roland B. Eutsler, now of the Wharton School at the University of Pennsylvania. The North Carolina Department of Agriculture study of all farmers in the state had showed the ratio of debt to value for mortgaged farms as 24.2 per cent. The study of Negro farm owners with mortgages showed a ratio of debt to value of 31.0 per cent. The chief sources of farm credit are insurance companies, holding 22.9 per cent of the total mortgages, Federal Land Banks (12.1 per cent), commercial banks (10.8 per cent), mortgage companies (10.4 per cent), joint stock land banks (7.0 per cent), individuals (29.6 per cent), and miscellaneous holders (7.2 per cent). Federal mortgage agencies occasionally make loans to Negro farmers but Federal Land Banks limit loans to members of loan associations. Negro farm owners are excluded from membership in white loan associations, and having formed none among themselves, are without these credits. Individuals hold 57 per cent of outstanding mortgages of Negroes as compared with 29.6 per cent for all farmers. The legal maximum of interest is 6 per cent, but various subterfuges resorted to often succeed in making this more.

The North Carolina Department of Agriculture study reported

70 per cent of the farmers using cash borrowings for their crop production needs. The average cost to owners was 7.6 per cent and to tenants 8.7 per cent. Seventy-nine per cent of the Negro farmers used short time cash loans. Banks supplied 80 per cent of the owners with credit and tenants received 65 per cent of their cash loans from landlords. A similar situation was observed by Dr. George Edmund Haynes, Director of the Inter-racial Commission of the Federal Council of Churches, who has just completed a survey of cotton growing communities in nine communities of four counties in Alabama. On short term credit the interest charges for the majority ranged from 15 to 19 per cent and in some cases it was even higher.

So long as working capital costs place such a heavy toll upon revenues from the sale of crops it is inconceivable that farm operations can yield a profit. Negro farmers in North Carolina generally use fertilizer and purchase it on credit. When the difference between the time and cash prices is adjusted for the length of the credit period, these Negroes pay about 37.2 per cent interest per year for fertilizer credit. The merchant credits averaged 39 per cent.

Merchants are almost the only credit agency which will grant loans for the whole of the crop season and covering all needs of the farmer. Seventy-five per cent of the total short-time credit among white farmers in North Carolina is supplied by merchants at an average cost of 25 per cent. Among Negro farmers one-third of the owners and two-thirds of the tenants received credits from time merchants. Both the Negro and white farmers originally depended upon merchant credit because of necessity and have continued to do so, thinks Dr. Eutsler, because of ignorance, lack of initiative or habit. There is a vicious circle with poor farming methods, lack of knowledge and education, concentration of production on cost crops, and methods of living being partially responsible for the dependence upon the high costs of merchant credit, while, on the other hand, these charges are partly responsible for continuing these conditions. Before there can be any improvement in the credit situation for Negro farmers, Dr. Eutsler thinks, they must improve their methods of production, their education and equipment, and they must restrict their borrowing to productive purposes only.

It is obvious, however, that these things cannot be done without money, or where all credit resources are needed for bare living. Likewise, it is obvious, as Dr. E. E. Lewis has pointed out, that if the Negro paid less in interest charges he would have more money left for himself. Improving the Negro's use of credit seems to involve not only a change in habit on the part of the farmer himself, but also an accompanying change in their whole economic situation. It is doubtful, indeed, if much will be accomplished by merely raising the Negro farmer to the level of the white farmer, for the prospects under the present system seem no brighter for one than for the other.

USES AND ABUSES OF FEDERAL FARM RELIEF

The final crisis in individual farm fortunes is reached when the Federal Government is forced to step in to avoid foreclosures and complete collapse. Federal aid has been available for farmers in the form of Feed, Seed and Fertilizer Loans, and through various agencies under the Reconstruction Finance Corporation. Although well conceived as an aid to relief, thay have not in practice escaped abuses of a notorious character insofar as Negro farmers are concerned. Not all of them have always been exploited, but the existence of abuses on so large a scale seems inexcusable in the administration of federal service in such desperate emergencies. Responsibility for a measure of this may be placed upon the unfortunate imperatives of the social system which regards the exploitation of Negroes as more or less a "normal" condition.

An illuminating account of these practices was revealed through investigations by Mr. W. W. Alexander of the Commission on Inter-racial Cooperation and his research aid, Dr. Arthur Raper, in counties in Georgia, Alabama and Mississippi. The Feed, Seed and Fertilizer Loans are designed to finance small farmers who otherwise could not plant a crop. The number of these loans has increased rapidly. In 1932, for example, about 44,000 of these loans were made in Georgia. In 1933, something near 100,000 will be made, this increase in number made possible by reduction of the individual loans and an increase in the amount available for loans. In numerous localities, well informed local people reported that there could be scarcely any farm operation without these loans, in other communities it is evident that solvent local planters and bankers put their own tenants on this loan service simply because they did not wish to take the risk involved in present farm operations.

The loans have been variously administered. In a few black belt areas tenants got and spent the loans made to them; they bought their feed, seed, and fertilizer at cash prices and accordingly had relatively smaller debts in the fall. The planters, however, usually got control of their tenants' checks through an oral agreement between the landlord and the tenant. As a matter of fact, the landlord virtually forces the tenant to deliver the check to him; the landlord explains to the tenant that he will not waive his rent to the government—one of the requirements for the loan—unless the tenant agrees to bring the check to him when it comes. When the tenant's check arrives he takes it to the landlord, and then and there either endorses it or, being unable to write his own name, "touches the pen," and the landlord endorses it for him. In some instances, the planter has taken the money and deposited it to his own account, issuing cash back to the tenant as he thought the tenant needed it. The planter usually charged 8 or 10 per cent interest. Thus, the tenant pays double interest—6 per cent to the Government for the money and an additional 8 or 10 per cent to the planter for keeping it for him! This practice is common in the upper part of the Georgia Black Belt.

The most expensive method, to the tenant, of administering the loan is when the planter secures the money from the tenant upon its arrival and then repays it to the tenant in feed, seed, and fertilizer at credit prices. This practice, which gives the tenant no benefit of cash prices, has been followed quite freely in the central Alabama Black Belt. These feed, seed and fertilizer loans to tenants actually provided the planters with the cash with which to buy feed, seed, and fertilizer at cash prices to be sold back to the tenants, who secured the loans, at time credit prices. It is the planter rather than the tenants, thus, who profits by these loans to the tenants.

In some black belt counties Negro landowners are not allowed to spend the cash which they secured through loans from the Government. In one Alabama county a merchant, who had taken over the check of a Negro who had secured a loan, said: "You know, it is not customary for niggers to get checks around here." The incident serves to illustrate the fact that Negro owners, too, move within the plantation practices of the community. Black belt Negro owners "know what they must do to make and keep their own ownership secure." Many Negro owners in black belt communities are far from being independent farmers.

There are numerous instances of flagrant violations of the Feed, Seed and Fertilizer Loan Service. Some planters have taken the loan money from their tenants and either applied most of it to old debts of their tenants, which is against the stipulations of the loans, or deposited it to their own accounts. Cases have been reported where planters secured money upon the names of Negro tenants who never received the money or knew of the loan that had been made in their names. Some of these cases came to light when the tenants received receipts from the Government for repaid loans of which they knew nothing. Several such cases have come into the courts, and a number of planters are now under sentence. It seems evident that this and similar practices of the planters involved the connivance of the local post office officials or letter carriers. Proof on this point, it seems, would not be difficult to ascertain. Known defrauds were not so common in the spring of 1933, or in 1932, as in 1931.

The Feed, Seed, and Fertilizer Loan and the Reconstruction Finance Corporation loan services have often failed in other ways to serve the Negro farm owners. The Reconstruction Finance Corporation farm loans are of large denominations and consequently not adapted to the small farmers of either race. Not infrequently, some local white merchant has desired to finance these owners, for the generous interest rates possible. This Government loan service is designed to aid those persons who could not otherwise finance their farm operations. There are instances of solvent planters who, after qualifying their own tenants for the loans by merely refusing to make advances to them, have sat on the county loan committees and disqualified Negro owners for the loans by volunteering to finance them. Financing these Negro owners, usually industrious and able to give valuable collateral for small loans, accords the planters an opportunity to make some profit from personal loans to them, whereas if cash were made available to these Negro owners through the Feed, Seed, and Fertilizer Loans, they would most likely do most of their cash trading at the larger stores.

Few black belt Georgia counties have secured R. F. C. funds, but in Alabama numbers of counties use this form of relief. The plantation is made the unit of distribution. Manipulations of highly questionable character are observed to be practiced and in most instances these have escaped even censure. For example, in an Alabama county where wages of 75 cents a day, one to three days a week, were being paid at the county seat, the local planter heading the county's R. F. C. work allowed only 50 cents a day per family one day a week in the rural part of the county. He did this, he asserts, to avoid disorganizing farm labor in his own community. Further, when spring came his fellow planters were able to get him to lower the wages from 75 to 50 cents a day at the county seat. There are instances of blacklisting of Negro R. F. C. laborers who were getting 50 cents a day, in order to force them to accept a planter's private offer of 35 cents a day.

The planter class appears to be proceeding upon the assumption that the landless farmer must be kept dependent. The propertyless tenants in turn have gotten all they could out of the owners before settlement time. Both are hard pressed, but the planter has a scapegoat.

Virtually the same type of irregularities appear in connection with relief provided by the American Red Cross. This service has kept many people alive during the past year, and during the winter months especially. Dr. Raper's investigations revealed that Red Cross service has been variously administered. In nearly all counties the plantation has been the unit of administration. Not infrequently, the plantation trucks carried the flour and cloth from the county seat to the plantation headquarters. Only in a few instances did the Negroes have any effective part in determining which families should receive Red Cross aid. The Negro Red Cross Chapter at Tuskegee, Macon County, Alabama, the only separate and distinct Negro Red Cross chapter in the United States, explains the active part taken by Negroes in that county. Also, the Red Cross service in the rural counties surrounding Montgomery has been administered more fairly than in most black belt counties. While local advisory Negro committees have had some influence in the direction of equalizing the services to the Negroes in some counties, as a general rule everything has been left to the county committee, usually composed of planters, merchants, and their agents.

There have been occasional flagrant abuses of the Red Cross service. In some communities flour and cloth have been used to feed and clothe families who have been stripped of their provisions by planters. "Let the Red Cross feed them," was what the planters could readily say after they had "cleaned out" their tenants. In one community the administrator of the Red Cross services is reported to have charged his tenants for the flour and cloth which "he secured" for them. It is impossible to estimate the proportion of the Red Cross' rations and cloth virtually "sold" to the tenants of the Black Belt. However, not all the accusations made against the planters are legitimate.

These abuses of the relief intended for the farmers reflect the weight of social tradition on the matter of the Negro and the least protected workers, perhaps, more than they reflect purely agricultural problems. It becomes a matter, in this instance, as in many others of the same order, of insuring the protection of this class of workers from abuses which are a part of the history of race relations in the section, before their normal plight as farmers can be effectively remedied.

THE OUTLOOK FOR AGRICULTURE

Even so restricted a question as credit for Negro farmers, when traced far enough, opens into monumental issues of international trade relations. For disregarding the special discomforts of the ultimate underdog, both white and Negro farmers are linked together in the system. "The outlook for agriculture," Dr. G. F. Warren of Cornell told the conference, "is the price outlook, and the outlook for prices is the outlook for the supply and demand for gold and the outlook for revaluation of the dollar and the amount of that revaluation." This point of view assumed the adequacy of the present economic organization for righting itself, so long as the relationship between supply and demand, and so far as value relationships could be restored.

This question of price levels and rates of increase of gold, however, Professor Edwin G. Nourse of Brookings Institute described as "metaphysical." Assuming that manipulation in our money currency could change the price level, "man doesn't pay his grocery bills with the price level." The analytical attack on money, he thought, should be made in terms of the place which money plays in our own system. Since gold reserves do not enter even into our Federal Reserve system in a bank, it is all the more strongly suggested that the standpoint of consideration of gold is that which reveals how it flows into the rest of our activity.

The agricultural situation lends itself to consideration in more tangible and realistic terms. Mr. Benjamin Hubert, for example, has advanced the notion of the necessity for a re-classification of lands. There seems to be little to induce large scale corporate farming in the southeast. The large capital outlays required in this type of farming and the low cost returns, he thought, would act as a discouragement. The risks are greater, both with respect to the competition of the sections for superior managerial ability, and with respect to the returns from the land. The area promises to be one of small farms, the size tending to group about 150 acres as the profitable unit. The small farmer, he thinks, may only expect to hold his own as he adopts a definite self-sufficiency program.

It seems clear, however, that there need be no thought of permanent improvement in agriculture until there have been radical changes in the system of land tenure. If there is to be tenantry it must be of such a character as to enable the tenant farm operator to share in whatsoever permanent improvements he has been able to make on the farm. At present many tenants are not good business risks and in most instances the landlord is not financially able to make advances to tenants. Usually when he is able he demands the right of general supervision. The destruction of the old plantation system will probably carry along with it the worst evils of the tenant system.

It is probable that some governmental assistance will be necessary for a while to permit the tenant more reasonable farm credits than are customary in the South, and along with this will go the necessity for supervision of this assistance to insure the Negroes in what it is intended that they should have.

Lands unfit for profitable farming should be abandoned. From one-third to two-fifths of all land in certain parts of the South could well be released to forests. According to H. H. Bennett, in charge of the soil erosion investigation for the United States Department of Agriculture, there are no less than 100,000 acres of land in one county in Northeast Georgia alone destroyed by erosion and abandoned.

Practically every study made of farming in the southeast shows that all other things being equal farmers who own and operate their farms have been most successful. The family farm will probably remain the dominant type of American agriculture. The one most frequent suggestion of a solution of the Negro farmers' difficulties has been that of land ownership. With farm lands exceedingly cheap it is believed that the Negro farmer might get lands which had previously been denied him for ownership. The objection here, valid enough, is that Negroes have no money with which to buy lands. Since white farmers, who were better situated than they economically, were being forced to abandon their own farms, it could scarcely be expected that the more severely impoverished Negroes could buy them.

The farm demonstration agents who have been regarded as educational influences in these farming communities, have a limited usefulness. Professor Eutsler feels that they are impotent at the present time because their salaries are paid partially by the communities or counties which employ them. And since the control of the counties is in the hands of the white group, any moves which threaten to interfere with the current practices of the white community are significantly frowned upon. Financial arrangements, one of the most acute points in Negro rural life, are excluded from the demonstrator's province.

Vocational education has also been suggested as a source of correction of the Negro farmers' plight. There is, however, the greatest uncertainty about the actual extent to which this is helping even the children of farmers. Only a small proportion of students in the land grant colleges are attracted by agricultural courses, a weakness which may be reflecting the hopeless unattractiveness of agriculture. Further, there are reflections in the attitude of the children of farmers of the unattractiveness of the courses, and a fundamental lack of interest in the field. It is urged, however, that more could be done in improving the teaching of agriculture. The courses have in many instances been so routinized and given such an intangible theoretical emphasis they swing free from all reality.

The farm land bank proposition which a short while ago was regarded as of especial usefulness to tenants, has not, according to Dr. George E. Haynes, helped the Negro tenants to any large extent. A proposal has been made to philanthropists to take over large areas and sub-divide them into small farms on long term amortizations and low interest rates. But it was admitted, in the very proposal, for such an extensive reorganization of agriculture as seems imperative, philanthropy can contribute but little and this perhaps only in the form of a demonstration.

The same fact of availability of large amounts of good farm land being held for sale by large financial corporations in default of mortgage payments has been suggested as a beginning for government or philanthropy in taking them over cheaply for re-distribution. This, again, is pointed out as a measure of restricted benefit.

For although the new tenants in such an experiment might be benefited, and the corporations pleased to rid themselves of the land, this same land represents the loss of home farms as well as larger areas by other thousands through the fundamental weaknesses in the system. These generally admitted weaknesses have drawn out expressions of hopelessness, of a disposition to turn attention to making the cities accommodate ultimately the masses of the population, expressions of the need for drastic governmental steps to protect the weaker elements of the farm population, through legislative control. Mr. James Ford of the Communist Party, for example, made two such proposals. One of them was that of compulsory unemployment insurance for agricultural workers which would guarantee to each head of a family $10.00 a week and $3 00 for each dependent. The other was cancellation of all farm mortgages. The virtual moratorium on mortgages in some sections of the South indicates, in a sense, a gesture in the direction of cancellation, although not wide enough to arouse the ultimate issues involved. These steps followed wholesale eventualities in individual loan situations amounting almost to collapse of the principle because of its general havoc. However, in the communities in question a vast amount of these mortgages were in the hands of non-local insurance companies and of banks. The ultimate destruction of values in mortgages would undoubtedly have some relationship to savings in the form of insurance and deposits on the basis of which insurance and bank loans are possible.

Still another proposal by Mr. Ford falls outside the governmental field. It is that of encouraging the organization of share croppers' unions. This seems merely an application of the principle of collective bargaining to agriculture. The chief objection to it would rest in the conservatism of the South regarding labor organization of any sort, a conservatism which has unquestionably permitted demoralization in wages and conditions of labor. The principle is accepted more largely in other sections of the country which are longer used to bargaining with labor.

The likelihood is that any such activity in the South or in unorganized agriculture would be given in the one instance a racial and in the other a political significance, which it did not wholly merit.

Finally, there is that factor which, despite its direct pertinence to the future of the Negro in agriculture yet has little surface relationship to economics. It has to do with the securing of rural

Negroes, not simply from poverty, but from physical violence. Dr. Arthur Raper says in a spirit of caution:

"When we are advocating the return—not merely the return to the farm but the permanent habitation—of these Negroes, we must remember that Negroes are nearly sixty times as much in danger of being lynched on a farm as in Atlanta or Birmingham or Houston or Dallas. The Negro does not have more than one-tenth to one-fortieth in school advantages, hospitalization advantages, public nurse advantages, in the rural community that he does in the urban center. In advocating home ownership we must develop some philosophy of inter-county, inter-state education, public welfare service, and some form of state police protection. Until something more is done in the direction of making equal the public welfares in these rural counties, it is a very hard thing to ask a man to go live there."

Something of the same consideration apparently was behind the even more impatient challenge of Dr. DuBois:

"Every time I hear the Negro farmer discussed I get mad. I want to throw things. I know that he faces the difficulties of all farmers today, but I know, too, that he faces more than that, he faces mob law, no schools, no vote, crop lien, usury and cheating. When a man discusses the Negro farmer and neglects or forgets to mention these facts I cannot believe in his sincerity! Of course, Negro farmers are stupid, slow and afraid—all the cream of swift intelligence, initiative and courage has run away or crawled away or lies murdered to fertilize southern soil."

The same inescapable sentiment might be read into the dispassionate and coldly phrased suggestion of Mr. Benjamin Hubert that:

"it seems inevitable that the independent Negro farm operator will eventually find it impracticable to continue to live in communities far removed from other members of his group. Constant daily contacts with members of his own group will make it possible for the Negro farmer to enjoy more of the real satisfactions of farm life."

Recognition of sentimental factors in the decline of the farm is not confined to the purely racial issue. The drabness of rural life and its remoteness from the centers of cultural growth has seemed important enough to prompt Mr. Edwin R. Embree, in a reflective mood, to question the value of a life that could only be supported at an ignoble level:

"The important question seems to me to be what the Negro may expect on the farm in the South. If he does not get lynched, what he seems to be assured of is merely the ability to support life. But he supports life at such an ignoble level, his face so constantly walked on by the lowest class above him, his economic position so often menaced by persons and conditions about him, that life on those terms, even if life continues, is not worth living by any group that calls itself human."

Such a philosophy minimizes even the ultimate ideal presented of the self-contained farm. No farm can be entirely self-contained, Mr. Embree insists. The machine and the division of labor are here and our standard of living depends almost entirely upon its use of the machine and the skillful division of labor. "Anyone who talks about giving these up," Mr. Embree said, "offers a return to the lowest possible standards of life."

The great and beautiful agrarian cultures of history, of which one hears so much sentimental talk, were all founded on slavery. That type of culture has gone forever, at least from the Western World. In place of human slaves, machines now do the drudging labor. The industrial revolution and scientific agriculture have brought in a new abundance while at the same time they have removed the need for much of the former hand drudgery. In the modern world a farmer is in little better position than the city man to provide directly by his own hands all the things he wants in food and clothes and shelter, to say nothing of common conveniences and luxuries. To suggest a return to self-sufficing farms is to propose giving up the modern standard of living and dropping back into primeval privation.

The deliberations of the Conference, linked themselves with current considerations of standards of living in relation to the actual productive capacity of our modern age. Instead of drastic and general curtailment of production, the new problem looms as one of under-consumption, which is the tragic correlate of a low living standard.

THE INDUSTRIAL FUTURE

By whatever fluctuations the status of Negroes was marked in industry the fact is ever evident that this status is bound up with the industrial fortunes of the country. A vague but ever present paradox exists wherever the subject is discussed, in the effort both to regard the Negro factor as an inseparable and fixed part of the whole, and to concentrate conspicuously on the Negro.

While the statistical implications of the 1930 census were that the Negro worker had maintained, as Professor Tyson noted in relation to steel "his sure foothold at the base of American industry," it was never quite apparent whether or not "base" was intended actually to mean "bottom." Since no unusual gains in industry were expected in such a distressed state of the industries as the present witnesses, the small absolute gains of Negroes in new lines over the past two decades was not surprising. The unanimity of the statistical evidence on the continued survival of the Negro worker was matched by a corresponding unanimity on the well-nigh inescapable low economic level of this survival. The testimony of all our industrial figures is that unemployment seeks the marginal worker, whether he is white but foreign-born, or too old, or whether he is black. The reflection in relief and emergency work roles of the uncounted but mounting volume of unemployment since 1930 forces the disconcerting conclusion that this racial differential could expand enormously, and to the increasing disadvantage of Negro workers. Without consciously intending it, the Conference found itself attacking the double problem of relieving the special distress of Negro workers, more helpless than the rest, and of improving their original industrial position. Early in the deliberations it was brought out that unlike most other working groups in America the economic future of the Negro is not in his own hands. There was little that he alone could do about it. This notion found forceful expression through President Mordecai Johnson of Howard University, when he said in somewhat general terms but nevertheless significantly:

> "The Negro must find his economic salvation in relation to the great, gigantic and collective operations that are going on and the central powers of which are outside his race."

Eleven per cent of all workers, set apart from the rest, even if they were of one mind or culture, could scarcely affect seriously the industrial future of the nation, although they could be a powerful minority factor in any given direction. Theirs is a contingent role.

Essentially the same notion was advanced in another light by Dr. DuBois, when he reminded the Conference that:

> "this matter of world depression and revolutionary changes in social life and industry is not primarily the problem of the American Negro, and just because it is not our problem we have plain proof of the thing that I said before, namely, that we are not in reality a part of this nation. We stand, even in its greatest crisis, at one side, only partially connected with its remedies, but dumb victims of its difficulties."

The notion of this enforced detachment, or helplessness was inescapable. Professor Kelly Miller detected it and made comment on it:

> "Throughout all our discussion there has been one undertone. It has not been so clearly expressed, but implied. That is the helplessness of the Negro in the midst of the depression and in the midst of the economic world by which he is surrounded."

Dr. Broadus Mitchell in course of his somewhat desperate speculation on the future of the American Negro referred to forces of "meteorologic uncontrollability" which have swept down upon us all:

> "The Negro has experienced these changes in the past. The introduction of the cotton gin which fostered slavery and cotton culture upon the southern states and upon the Negro; the migration during the World War, the great changes in technology which have altered our whole economic science, and the present depression—these are natural forces or at any rate objective forces which are indomitable apparently. They take our efforts, our most cherished schemes, our highest ideals, and in this case make them into nothing."

As a minority group the Negro has been able to hold a position in industry and in the economic order, Dr. Frazier asserted, only as he has been able to function most efficiently as that economic unit. In the history of the country, white servitude in Pennsylvania drove out Negro slaves, and it had little to do with individual or group kindness. In Virginia, Negro slavery drove out white servitude as a similarly competing economic force.

GENERAL FINDINGS

Analysis of the discussions reveals clearly several universes of discourse, and the remedies suggested followed this division. No satisfactory composite of the thinking of the group seems possible. There were those who in consciousness of weakness, would appeal to the strength of dominant industry, to the enlightened self-interest of individual employers, and to the conscience of the nation. There were others who would challenge the human idealism in employers, or, in a spirit of moral challenge offer to them a last chance to discover whether "in addition to the love of profits they have sufficient love of humankind, poor whites and black alike, to organize industry with the cooperation of the Federal Government in such a way as to give ordinary employment and everyday security to the humble people of the nation." There were those who looked to the power of religion, or at least the influence of the Church, and those who felt that "the church cannot be the Negro's salvator, since it can hardly save itself." There were those who envisioned again the self-sufficiency of a separate state, "where Negroes could develop unimpaired, however many mistakes were made, or however slow the development, so long as it would be their development and their civilization." And there were those who condemned such dreams as desperate folly belonging to the 17th century. Programists saw in the freedom of Negroes from the guilt of exploitation, and in their long history of back-breaking labor, "a chance to give the world an example of intelligent economic cooperation so that when the new industrial commonwealth comes we can go into it as an experienced people and not again be left on the outside as mere beggars." Others, convinced that no patching of a wretchedly defective system can do more than palliate and lull men's intelligences to sleep, called for a redistribution of wealth and complete socialization of the processes of consumption and distribution of production. Some wanted gradual socialization and peaceful revolution, there were others who felt that violent, sudden and complete revolution could be no worse than what we are now witnessing. These were advocates of cooperative measures, of education, of voting, or propaganda, of good will, of watchful waiting, and of faith. The diversity served to portray that most bewildering of situations in which there is utter certainty of the evil and utter uncertainty of the cure.

Earlier conferences have concerned themselves item by item with corrective measures. This Conference thought predominantly in terms of panaceas, utterly irreconcilable among themselves.

A point on which there was virtual unanimity was that of the delecterous operation of the factor of race prejudice which, in its subtle pervasiveness, so often planted barriers to personal comfort and to social justice.

The proposal was advanced by Dr. Paul Douglas that the Negro might use his bargaining power as a group with organized labor. He suggested that we are probably going to have from the new administration industrial legislation of far-reaching nature. If the Sherman Anti-Trust Act is waived in connection with certain industries which organized themselves to regulate production, in return for this is expected the counter provisions of minimum wages and maximum hours, or in other words, some degree of recognition of unionism. Just as employers pay the price for combinations the unions should be made to pay the price of abolishment of racial discrimination.

Vocational guidance as a means of control over the situation was advanced repeatedly. Mr. T. Arnold Hill expressed it in terms of re-training workers.

Unquestionably capacity will play a large part in the selection of workers for the new era. The depression has given employers the opportunity to select the best of the unemployed. Machinery will now do many of the unskilled tasks formerly performed by man. Industry's big problem is not production but distribution, and the large number of unemployed trained people competing for jobs permits selection on the basis of individual fitness.

There is nothing definite to indicate the precise training that American workers should be given to equip them for a particular industry or type of work in the future. Educational philosophies expound the theory of re-training but they must await the expanse of business before they can determine what sort of education should be emphasized.

Nevertheless considerable re-training is provided by private organizations, state and city governments as a relief measure. There is a real chance for all workers to develop skills and talents in connection with emergency schools and colleges such as there are in New York and Ohio. In rural areas of the South home demonstration provides instruction in canning and weaving. This type of instruction permits adult workers to explore their potentialities; for a wide variety of artistic and cultural subjects as well as manual trades is offered.

We have seen in the field of selling and marketing examples of how Negroes may be used in new experiments. Something akin to an experimental laboratory in an industrial plant must be developed to find uses for the hordes of our young people who cannot find adequate outlet for their talents. As we have found new uses for food products, as wagon companies have scrapped their old equipment in order to build automobiles; and as established industrial corporations have developed by-products from their main products, so must somewhere in the machinery which is concerned with the employment problems of Negroes provision be made to experiment with colored youth in untried fields.

There has been some fairly successful experimentation in the field of guidance. Mr. Franklin Keller of the National Occupational Conference reported on recent work in New York. Faced with a blind alley for Negro youth finishing northern high schools, they made a study in New York City which revealed a wide range of hitherto unsuspected occupational opportunities for Negroes. As a result of this they formulated a set of recommendations for the New York Public Schools. They were that:

1. Negro boys and girls should be admitted to vocational schools on the same basis as white children.

2. All school persons should have authentic information regarding Negroes in occupations.

3 Every effort should be made by counselors to induce employers to take a more liberal attitude toward Negro workers

4. All counselors should be assigned for specific periods to visit industry and business.

5 Counselors in Negro districts should be selected for their special knowledge of the Negro situation.

6. The material in this survey should be kept up to date and should be amplified by staff members released for the purpose.

7. Every method should be made to enforce strictly the attendance laws as they affect Negro children, especially between fifteen and seventeen years of age.

8. A sufficient number of junior high schools should be organized in Negro districts to accommodate all children of junior high school age.

9. A central guidance bureau for adults should be established in the Harlem district.

10. The Board of Education should continue to work out the problems of Negro education in cooperation with the bi-racial advisory committee which has cooperated in this survey.

Proposals for the next steps to be taken yielded broad suggestions. Mr. Eugene Kinckle Jones of the National Urban League offered a platform for a free association of social and economic measures. He set as goals to be accomplished by or on behalf of the Negro the decentralization of the Negro population, with intelligent direction or control of migration and interpretation of employment needs of localities to Negroes; more diversification of employment among Negroes; adequate programs for the constructive use of leisure time; removal of the inferiority complex of Negroes in regard to economic status by convincing the group that their potentialities are as great as any other group; securing for Negroes of the benefits of social insurance, improvement of vocational guidance including the use of some such method as is developed in the Antioch plan; more adequate educational facilities in the South for Negroes to train for the professions; recognition of Negro labor by organized labor; relief in unemployment crises on the basis of need rather than population; raising of health standards; and development of a type of leadership depending more on training than on experience.

The machinery by which this might be accomplished includes suggestions of an interesting type. The main efforts to help the Negro economically, Mr. Jones thinks, must be assumed by the national government. Negroes should be on the staffs of government departments. Private agencies whose work affects Negroes should examine their programs to the view of functioning more adequately to obtain these ends. To attain these goals new departments or agencies are essential. There should be a fund for financing especially gifted or talented youth; an adequately financed nation-wide health program; and a fund should be raised by Negroes themselves to test the legality of unfair division of school funds in the South.

Dr. W. E. B. DuBois, in offering suggestions under the same heading, proposed what he termed revolutionizing changes: the abandonment of the profit idea; the conservation of the Negro family for sheer physical survival of the best; the shifting of emphasis from production to consumption, and work primarily for service rather than profit.

The wide difference in points of view expressed throughout the discussion of the Conference revealed an uncertainty regarding remedy, which was as acute as the uncertainty of status. It was clear, however, that American Negro labor, though unique in many respects, was so intricately bound up with the fate of American labor generally that any consideration of future programs must have fundamental relationship to the program for all labor. For closer study of the factual data and the contributions from the experience of various members of the Conference, a special committee was created. This committee attempted to formulate the sentiments of the Conference and project certain of these as general proposals and plans for immediate action.

SUMMARY OF FACTUAL DATA PRESENTED
TO THE CONFERENCE

POPULATION

1. Numerically the Negro has increased 58 per cent since 1890.
2. Proportionately the Negro decreased from 11.9 per cent of the total population in 1890 to 9.7 per cent in 1930.
3. Negroes in rural areas increased 11.5 per cent between 1890 and 1930.
4. Negroes in urban areas increased 250.7 per cent between 1890 and 1930.
5. The trend of Negro population followed the direction of cotton development from 1890 to the period of the world war.
6. There has been a decline in the "true rate of natural increase" among Negroes in the last ten years.
7. Percentages of Negroes in cities of over 250,000 have increased while percentages of Negroes in rural communities have decreased.
8. Between 1890 and 1930 percentages of Negroes in age groups below twenty have decreased and those above twenty have increased.
9. The proportion of Negroes living in the northern states increased 10 per cent between 1910 and 1930.

THE SOUTH

1. The business recession in the South began earlier than in the nation generally.
2. Money incomes in the South are chronically lower by approximately one-third than the national average.
3. Southern agriculture is devoted primarily to the production of goods for export and not foodstuffs.
4. Incomes from southern cotton crops declined tremendously between 1929 and 1932.
5. Southern population showed a further shift from rural to urban areas between 1920 and 1930.
6. Among the manufacturing industries in the South, the iron and steel industry has been most seriously affected.

[43]

7. The southern division of the textile industry has maintained volume but with demoralization of prices, wages, employment, and profits.
8. Coal mining and the production of petroleum output has sustained physical volume with price and wage demoralization.
9. Ninety per cent of the former lumber market had dried up in 1932.

OCCUPATIONAL DISTRIBUTION OF NEGROES

1. The percentage of Negroes gainfully employed increased from 41.0 per cent in 1890 to 46.3 per cent in 1930.
2. Changes in percentages of Negroes in occupational divisions have been:

	1890	1930
Agriculture	56.6	36.7
Domestic and Personal Service	31.2	28.6
All other	13.0	34.7

3. The per cent of Negroes gainfully employed increased 79 per cent between 1890 and 1930.
4. Negroes in manufacturing and mechanical industries increased 492.4 per cent between 1890 and 1930, but upon a relatively small numerical base.
5. Negroes in transportation and communication increased 260.1 per cent between 1890 and 1930, but upon a relatively small numerical base.
6. The number of Negroes in trade increased 535.8 per cent between 1890 and 1930, also upon a relatively small numerical base.
7. Negroes in professional service increased 313.4 per cent.
8. The occupational trends of Negro males have been similar North and South from 1910 to 1930 except in the case of domestic and personal service.
9. The occupational status of Negro women in the North has not changed in twenty years. In the South there has been a change from agriculture to domestic and personal service.

AGRICULTURE

1. The outlook for agriculture at the present time is better than it has been at any time in four years.
2. The trend toward unprofitable farming in South Carolina, Georgia, Alabama, and Mississippi has continued for 25 years.
3. Southern cotton production is exceeding the demand.

4. There is a production shortage in food and feed crops in the South.
5. Negro land owners and tenants decreased in South Carolina, Georgia, Alabama, and Mississippi between 1920 and 1930.
6. The southern credit system has no advantage for the debtor.
7. The ratio of debt to value of mortgaged farms in North Carolina where a significant study of this factor has been made, was higher for Negroes than for whites.
8. Seventy-nine per cent of the Negro farmers in North Carolina use short time cash loans.
9. Working capital costs place such a heavy toll upon revenues from the sale of crops it is inconceivable that farm operators can yield a profit.
10. Working capital costs for whites is inordinately high in North Carolina but even higher for Negroes.
11. Costs of loans to farmers in North Carolina generally exceed the legal level.
12. Mortgages in Alabama and Georgia require that the borrower waive his homestead rights to the minimum.
13. Federal aid through relief agencies in the South due to southern control of them does not aid the tenant and the Negro farmer. The planter by fair means or foul secures the benefits for himself.

MINING

1. The peak of coal production was reached in 1918.
2. Coal production in 1932 was at the lowest level it has been in thirty years.
3. The number of miners increased from 1890 to 1923 and has constantly decreased since.
4. The coal industry expanded after 1918 without consideration of the coal demand.
5. Two hundred thousand miners must be withdrawn from the industry to improve wages.
6. Negroes were 8.1 per cent of bituminous coal miners in 1920, the bulk of them being in Alabama, West Virginia, and Kentucky.
7. Mechanization of the mines making for technological unemployment is taking place despite the objections of miners.
8. Negro miners have not as yet been affected by mechanization to any considerable extent in the southern mines.

A. Food Products

1. Few Negroes have been employed in the food products industry and those largely as unskilled workers.
2. The breweries, revived for the manufacture of beer, do not employ Negroes.

B. Iron, Steel, and Machinery

1. The Negro's percentage of employees in iron, steel, and machinery industries increased slightly between 1920 and 1930, while there was a decrease in total employment.
2. Negro industrial employment is concentrated in the fields of durable goods production that have been most curtailed.
3. The increase in unemployment among laborers between April, 1930, and January, 1931, was greatest among Negroes.
4. Among the steel workers Negroes and native whites showed an equal amount of unemployment less than that of foreign-born whites.

C. Skilled Crafts and Construction

1. Lines in which Negro artisans and craftsmen have been developing have been declining due to concentration in factories and technological changes.
2. The importance of carpenters and draftsmen in the building industry has been diminished.
3. Negro carpenters declined absolutely and relatively between 1920 and 1930.
4. The decline of Negro machinists between 1920 and 1930 was greater than the decline of machinists as a whole.
5. Since 1890 Negroes have gained in masonry, iron working, and stationary engineering, and have lost ground in carpentry, plastering, brick and tile making, marble and stone cutting, blacksmithing, wheelwrighting, boot and shoemaking, harness and saddle making, leather currying and tanning.
6. Negro carpenters, bricklayers, and contractors have been displaced on a large scale by white workers in the South.
7. Negro artisans and building trade craftsmen provide only one-third of their proportion of the population.
8 The most consistent losses of Negro artisans are in the group

of crafts which are diminished in importance, and in carpentry.

9. The proportion of Negroes in the skilled fields remained about the same between 1920 and 1930.
10. The largest concentration of Negroes under manufacturing and mechanical industries is to be found in the building industry.
11. The group with the highest unemployment rate, according to the 1930 unemployment census, was building laborers.
12. The Negro bricklayers, roofers and slaters, electricians, plasterers, building contractors, and cabinet makers showed smaller increases than the total in the 1930 census.
13. Negro plumbers, painters, and cement finishers showed greater increases than the total.
14. The figures for the rate of increase of Negro molders was greater than the figures for the total molders declined.
15. White tool makers increased more than the Negro tool makers declined.
16. In the waning or dying crafts the decline of the total was twice as rapid as that of Negroes.
17. In new occupational fields Negro skilled workers increased 13.6 per cent.
18. The Negro rate of increase in industry is due to the industrialization following the World War and the northward migration of Negroes.

PROFESSIONAL SERVICE AND BUSINESS

1. Negro retail places, restaurants, cafes, lunch rooms, and lodging houses increased between 1920-1930.
2. The Negro financial groups doubled within the same period.
3. Negro clerical employment increased between 1920 and 1930.
4 Commercial classes, insurance, automotive transportation, positions of management in manufacturing and mechanical enterprises increased.
5. The problem in the professional classes is not one of over-population but one of maldistribution.
6. Negro professional classes increased 69 per cent between 1920 and 1930, but the ratio of professionals to the population is yet considerably less than the white population.
7. In the ministry alone Negroes have fewer persons per professional than the white population.

8. Salaried and fee workers, and entrepreneurs have suffered diminished incomes during recent years, due to the financial condition of their clientele.
9. Banking and insurance have suffered serious declines since 1930.

1. Negro women are 9.7 per cent of the woman population 10 years of age and over.
2. They are 17.1 per cent of employed women.
3. The percentage of Negro women employed is higher than the percentage of white women employed.
4. From 1920 to 1930 the number of Negro women employed grew rapidly with a slight increase in their proportion to the total.
5. The largest number of Negro women, according to the 1930 census, were employed in agriculture and domestic and personal service.
6. Negro women decreased in agriculture but increased in domestic and personal service.
7. The number of Negro women in manufacturing industries declined between 1920 and 1930.
8. Negro dressmakers, seamstresses and cigar and tobacco factory workers contribute the largest groups of Negro women in manufacturing industries. Employment in these fields declined, but the decline was greater for white than for Negro women.
9. Increases in food and clothing industries were greater for Negro women than white women.
10. Negro women are 45 per cent of the entire Negro professional classes, being four-fifths of all school teachers, librarians, social and welfare workers, and one-half of the actors and artists.
11. In the depression Negro women showed the highest unemployment rates.

PAPERS AND PARTICIPANTS

This report is based upon the following papers presented and read before the Conference on the Economic Status of the Negro:

POPULATION AND OCCUPATION TRENDS OF THE NEGRO: 1890-1930.
Monroe Work, Director, Department of Records and Research, Tuskegee Institute.
P. K. Whelpton, Scripps Foundation for Research in Population Problems.

NEGRO WORKERS IN SKILLED CRAFTS AND CONSTRUCTION.
Charles S. Johnson, Director, Department of Social Science, Fisk University.

THE RELATION OF THE NEGRO TO EMPLOYMENT AND UNEMPLOYMENT IN THE STEEL AND MACHINERY INDUSTRIES.
Francis D. Tyson, Professor of Economics, University of Pittsburgh.

THE RELATION OF THE NEGRO TO UNEMPLOYMENT IN FOOD PRODUCTS.
Maurice Moss, Executive Secretary, Urban League, Pittsburgh, Pennsylvania.

THE RELATION OF THE NEGRO TO THE UNEMPLOYMENT SITUATION IN THE BITUMINOUS COAL INDUSTRY.
Homer L. Morris, Professor of Economics, Fisk University.

DISORGANIZATION TO SOUTHERN INDUSTRY BROUGHT ON BY THE DEPRESSION.
Claudius T. Murchison, Professor of Applied Economics, University of North Carolina.

THE IMPACT OF INDUSTRIAL UNEMPLOYMENT OF THE NEGRO:
Joseph H. Willits, Professor of Industry; Director of the Wharton School of Finance, University of Pennsylvania.

THE FUTURE OF THE NEGRO IN AMERICA.
Broadus Mitchell, Professor of Political Economy, Johns Hopkins University.

HUMAN FACTORS IN THE DISPLACEMENT AND REEMPLOYMENT OF NEGRO WORKERS.
T. Arnold Hill, Director, Department of Industrial Relations, National Urban League.

THE NEGRO AT WORK IN NEW YORK CITY.
Franklin J. Keller, Director, National Occupational Conference, New York City.

INDUSTRIAL EMPLOYMENT OF NEGRO WOMEN.
Mary Anderson, Director, Women's Bureau, U. S. Department of Labor.

DISORGANIZATION OF THE NEGRO FAMILY BROUGHT ON BY THE DEPRESSION.
E. Franklin Frazier, Professor of Sociology, Fisk University.

SOME HEALTH PROBLEMS OF THE NEGRO.
Dr. M. O. Bousfield, President, Supreme-Liberty Life Insurance Company, Chicago, Illinois.

THE OUTLOOK FOR AGRICULTURE.
G. F. Warren, Professor of Agricultural Economics and Farm Management, Cornell University.
Edwin G. Nourse, Institute of Economics, Washington. D. C.

ADJUSTMENT AND COOPERATION NEEDED IN THE RELATION OF CREDIT AGENCIES TO THE NEGRO FARM OWNER, TENANT, AND SHARE-CROPPER.
Roland B. Eutsler, Instructor in Industry, Wharton School of Finance and Commerce, University of Pennsylvania.

THE FUTURE OF THE NEGRO IN COTTON DEVELOPMENT IN THE SOUTH.
Edward E. Lewis, Assistant Professor of Economics, Howard University.

THE ECONOMIC STATUS OF THE NEGRO IN BUSINESS AND THE PROFESSIONS.
Ira DeA. Reid, Director, Department of Research, National Urban League.

RACE RELATIONS AND ECONOMICS.
Will W. Alexander, Director, Commission on Interracial Cooperation; President, Dillard University.
Arthur Raper, Commission on Interracial Cooperation.

THE ROLE OF THE SMALL SOUTHERN FARM IN THE FUTURE LAND UTILIZATION PROGRAM.
B. F. Hubert, President, Georgia State Industrial College.

THE NEXT STEPS.
W. E. B. DuBois, Editor, *The Crisis*, National Association for the Advancement of Colored People.
Eugene Kinckle Jones, Executive Secretary, National Urban League.

A NEW ERA IN ECONOMICS AND CULTURE.
Edwin R. Embree, President, Julius Rosenwald Fund.

Paul H. Douglas, Professor of Economics, University of Chicago.

Kelly Miller, Professor of Sociology, Howard University.

Wm. J. Cooper, Commissioner of Education.

James H. Dillard, formerly of the Jeanes and Slater Funds.

George E. Haynes, Director, Interracial Commission, Federal Council of Churches; Director Cotton Survey Conference, Alabama, Arkansas, Mississippi.

Mordecai Johnson, President, Howard University.

Otto Geier, Cincinnati Milling Machine Company.

Walter Hill, General Education Board.

John M. Gandy, President, Virginia State College.

Mary McLeod Bethune, President, Bethune-Cookman College.

Alfred K. Stern, Julius Rosenwald Fund.

Louis Brownlow, Director, Public Administration Clearing House, Chicago.

Channing H. Tobias, National Council of the Young Men's Christian Associations.

Herman Feldman, Dartmouth College.

REPORT OF THE SPECIAL COMMITTEE OF THE CONFERENCE ON THE ECONOMIC STATUS OF THE NEGRO

1. The economic future of the Negro worker is linked with the economic future of American labor generally. Although Negro workers are held below the level of American labor generally neither group has attained under the present system an adequate standard of living. The greatest and most far reaching improvement of Negro labor will come as the gains of democracy are broadly distributed among all people.

2. The right to bargain collectively for the protection of the interests of those who labor belongs to those who labor, black and white alike. But any conferring of further power or privilege upon organized labor so long as it excludes or discriminates against other workers is a danger both to organized labor and to the excluded or unorganized black labor, and is to be avoided.

3. The great productive capacity of the country, which is responsible for a surplus of goods should not be restricted merely to keep up the price level but this capacity should be more adequately utilized through wider consumption, which would be made possible by greater purchasing power among wage-earners and which would contribute to a universal elevation of the living level.

4. Agriculture cannot be improved nor the Negro nor white farmer benefited until the present tenant and credit systems have been radically reorganized and on a basis which offers greater independence and sharing by the tenant of his own improvements on the land, and which permits terms of credit, which do not exploit the tenant and which give the tenant an opportunity to purchase his own farm.

5. The Federal Government is obligated in such an emergency as the present not merely to assist in making relief available for those helplessly stranded through unemployment or agricultural disaster, but to insure, through direct and cautious supervision, that this aid shall be distributed justly and not, as has been the case, in some localities with partiality and injustice. The Government likewise has the opportunity to encourage, or support further constructive programs of assistance for its economically handicapped citizens.

6. Social and economic planning are necessary and should be used to the end of adjusting our productive capacity to universally improved standards of living.

7. No separate salvation is possible or expected for Negro workers, but no improvement of the status of American workers should be considered without the full inclusion of Negro workers.

8. Just as there can be no separate economic redemption, there can be no lasting economic improvement without a corresponding social improvement.

The Committee's recommendations for immediate and specific action are:

1. The calling of regional economic conferences for the study and formation of plans for securing and improving the position of Negroes both in industry and in agriculture.

2. A further investigation of federal relief to Negroes through the Feed, Seed and Fertilizer Loans, the various agencies of the Reconstruction Finance Corporation, reforestation projects and public work programs.

3. Insistence upon more direct and impartial supervision of Federal relief measures.

4. Recommendation of competent Negroes, to be drawn from such services as the Smith-Hughes and Smith Lever programs, from the staffs of Negro agricultural colleges and other institutions or agencies of similar character, for those branches of the Federal relief service which have special importance for Negroes.

5. The Committee urges Negro farmers to enter into cooperative agricultural enterprises wherever possible.

6. The Committee recommends that in the administration of agricultural benefits, the United States Employment Exchanges, and such other national programs as the Tennessee Valley Authority, effort be made to utilize Negroes, some of whom, as for example the Farm Demonstration Agents, are peculiarly fitted to serve with leadership in such a capacity.

7. The Committee recommends that the basis of any agreement between capital and labor, under the sponsorship of the government, should include the provision that there be no discrimination on account of race or color.

8. In view of the increasing importance of the Negro vote, which is no longer expressed through a single party, opportunity is at hand for Negroes to participate more directly in the determination of governmental policies.

It was the feeling of the Committee that the chief and surest programs on behalf of Negroes involve both their original education and re-education, and persistent labors to help them provide for themselves a surer economic base upon which they may, on their own initiative and in the freedom and satisfaction of economic security, protect their health, secure their homes, educate their children, and live their own lives, unenvious and unenvied, in peace with their fellows.

Committee:

CHARLES S. JOHNSON, *Chairman*
W. W. ALEXANDER
GEORGE C. CLEMENTS
T. ARNOLD HILL
KELLY MILLER
BROADUS MITCHELL
R. R. MOTON
WALTER WHITE

CPSIA information can be obtained
at www.ICGtesting.com
Printed in the USA
LVHW031511020519
616417LV00012B/602/P